The United States Has Rules and Laws

Chad Taylor

Rosen Classroom
New York

My name is Hank.

I arrive at school on time.

This is a school rule.

This is my teacher, Mr. Jones. He is teaching us about rules and laws.

Mr. Jones says that people make rules. Teachers in our school make rules. We get in trouble if we do not follow rules.

My classmate was texting
during class.
This is against the rules.
The teacher took her phone away.

Mr. Jones says that the U.S.
government makes laws.
We learn about federal laws.
Federal laws apply to
all 50 states.

Federal laws start as bills.
Then they become laws.
Bills become laws when they are signed by the president.

Immigration laws are
federal laws.
These laws are for people who
want to become U.S. citizens.

States have their own laws, too.
They are called state laws.
Many driving laws are state laws.

People get in trouble
if they break laws.
This driver was driving too fast.
He gets a speeding ticket
from a policeman.

Police officers make sure people follow laws.
It is important to follow laws.
Laws keep people safe.

Words to Know

bills

driving laws

immigration laws

police officers

states

teacher